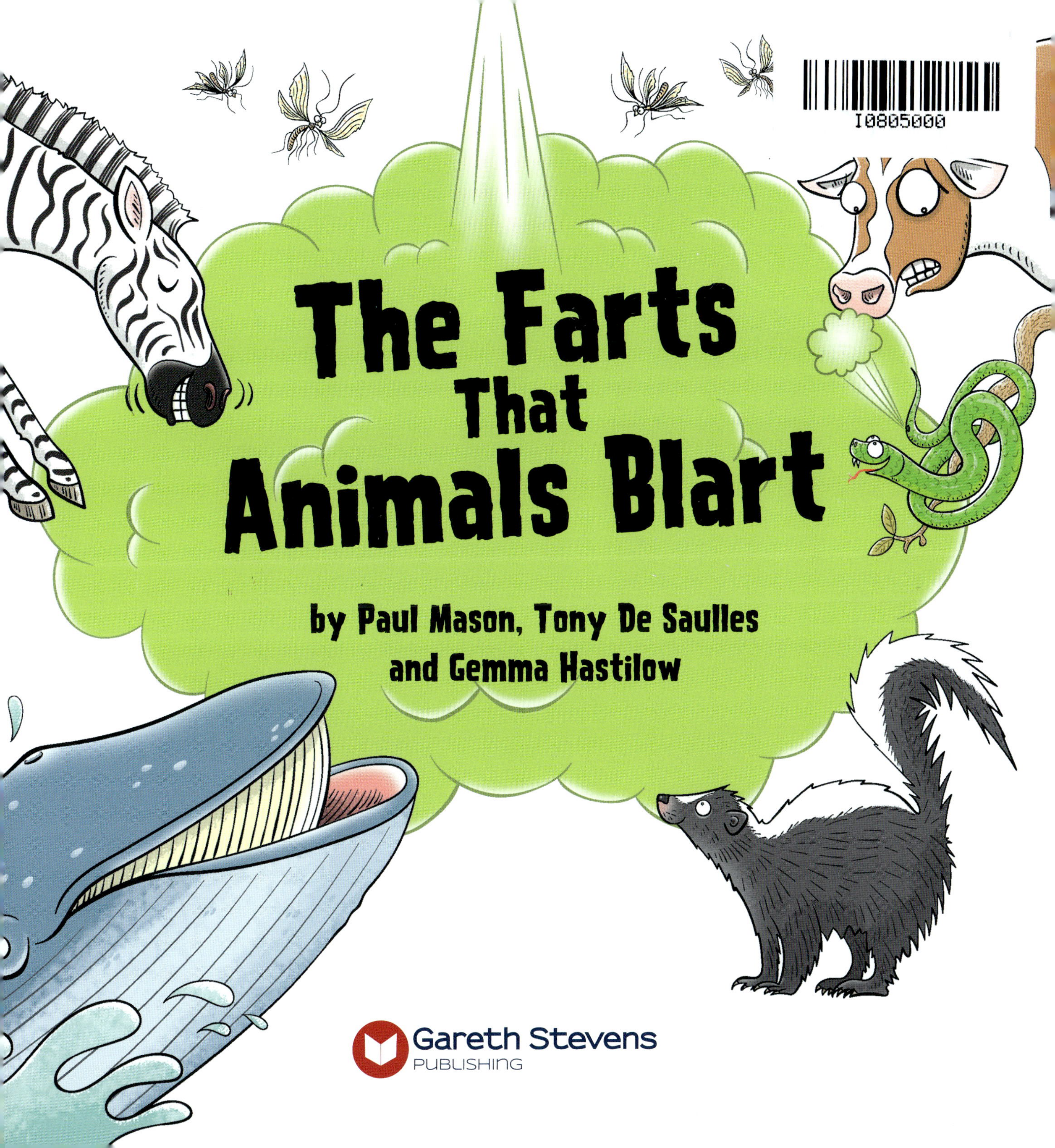

The Farts That Animals Blart

by Paul Mason, Tony De Saulles and Gemma Hastilow

Gareth Stevens Publishing

Please visit our website, www.garethstevens.com. For a free color catalog of all our high-quality books, call toll free 1-800-542-2595 or fax 1-877-542-2596.

Cataloging-in-Publication Data
Names: Mason, Paul, 1967-, author. | De Saulles, Tony, illustrator. | Hastilow, Gemma, illustrator.
Title: The farts that animals blart / by Paul Mason, illustrated by Tony De Saulles and Gemma Hastilow.
Description: Buffalo, NY : Gareth Stevens Publishing, 2026. | Series: What animals do | Includes glossary and index.
Identifiers: ISBN 9781482473421 (pbk.) | ISBN 9781482473438 (library bound) | ISBN 9781482473445 (ebook)
Subjects: LCSH: Animal behavior--Juvenile literature. | Flatulence--Juvenile literature.
Classification: LCC QL751.5 M376 2026 | DDC 591.5--dc23

Published in 2026 by
Gareth Stevens Publishing
2544 Clinton St.
Buffalo, NY 14224

First published in Great Britain in 2020 by Wayland

Editors: Grace Glendinning and Melanie Palmer
Designers: Peter Scoulding and Cathryn Gilbert

Picture credits:
Photo of Milo used with kind permission of Jono Goldsack and Lucy Rubenstein:14.
Photo of Bolson pupfish used with kind permission of Johnny Jensen, JJPhoto.dk, aquariumphoto.dk: 12.
Shutterstock: Aleksi Alekhin 18; Andrissimo 29; Kurit Ashfen 23b; Bamgraphy 7t; Seyms Brugger 15; Chameleons Eye 21b; Ch123 23c; Couperfield 19; Cpaulfell 21c; Claude Huot 6; IrinaK 9;C Jansuebsri 5cr; dejan_k 16; Ryosuke Kuwahara 5br; Lehrer 20; MicheleB 28; Teresa Moore 24; Parkol 25; RZ_Videos 7b; james_stone 76 5tr; Viper345 8; John Woolwerth 13.

Printed in the United States of America

CPSIA compliance information: Batch #CSGS26: For further information contact Gareth Stevens at 1-800-542-2595.

Contents

Welcome to FLATOLOGY

Your first question is probably, "What IS flatology?" It is the study of "flatulence" – the scientific name for farts.

Animals, including humans, have happily (and unhappily) broken wind for millennia. Farts even feature in the world's oldest known joke, written on a Sumerian tablet carved almost 4,000 years ago:

> "Something that has never occurred since time began: a young woman did not fart in her husband's lap."

OK, it's not very funny – but maybe humor was different back then.

Time for some SCIENCE ...

What's in a fart?

Farts are made up of many gases. The amount of each changes, depending on what you eat. The amount of nitrogen in a human fart can be 20–90 percent.

Hydrogen sulfide gas gives farts that eggy smell. It makes up only 1 percent of most human farts.

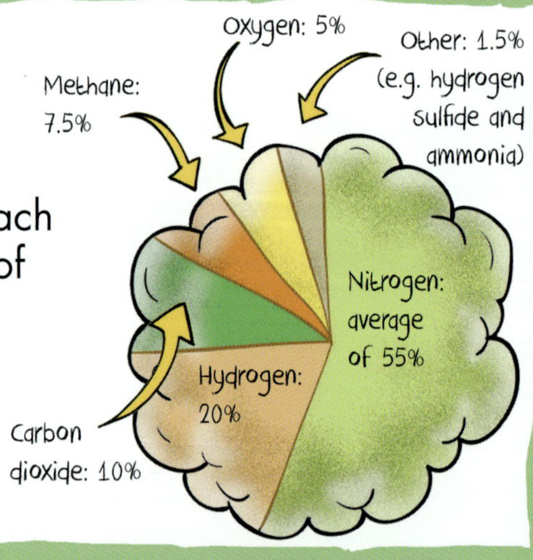

Just what is a fart?

A scientist would describe flatulence as "gases produced during digestion, combined with air." It goes like this:

1. Food reaches an animal's intestines.

2. Bacteria break it down into nutrients to be absorbed into the animal's blood.

3. Some of these bacteria produce gases as they work.

4. The gases are later released – almost always by being farted out through the animal's bottom.

Flatulence might be noisy, it might not.

It could be smelly, but maybe not.

It might even be silent, but deadly.

(Literally! Read on to find out about beaded lacewing larvae's killer farts.)

A FART IN OTHER WORDS

There is a word for "fart" in just about every language. Here is a selection from around the world – just in case you have a wind problem while traveling:

Hawaiian: *oi aku*
Uzbek: *osma*
Maori: *tutaki*
German: *furz*

The animal world's biggest FARTERS

Which farters are the biggest? This is not as easy to answer as you might think: it depends on what you mean by big.

Witnesses have said that the blue whale's digestive gases are revolting: "an unholy mixture of fart and fishiness."

Giant whale farts?

Bigger animals usually equal bigger farts. But, although some whales are huge, they may not do the world's biggest farts. Whale farts probably bubble out in little bits, rather than one massive trumpet. Whales also get rid of some digestive gases through their blowholes in giant, fishy belches.

Endurance farting

Hippos do some of nature's longest-lasting farts. When a hippo feels threatened, it aims its bottom at you and does an enormous *faaaaaart.* At the same time, it poops and whirs its tail like a fan, jet-spraying poop all over. They have been recorded doing noisy poop sprays for about 11 seconds*.

*If 11 seconds doesn't sound that long, go and stand behind a poop-spraying hippo ...

Termites don't fart big, but there are billions and billions of them. They are thought to fart out roughly 10 percent of the world's methane each year.

Tiny (but plentiful) farter

If "big" means "the most gas produced as a species," the world's biggest farter is one of its smallest animals: the termite. Together, the world's termites are thought to produce about 22 million tons (20 million mt) of methane each year.

Death by farts

The world is protected against termite farts partly by an insect called the beaded lacewing. The lacewing larvae hang around termite mounds and hunt termites using what's thought to be the world's only killer fart. It contains a chemical called allomone, which paralyzes, then kills, termites. Now that is a powerful fart.

Can a python Fart?

You'd know the answer to this if you had ever stood next to a python for long. Yes: pythons do some of the stinkiest farts in the animal kingdom.

Meaty farter

Animals that eat a lot of meat, such as pythons, do some of the worst-smelling farts. This is because fatty meat contains a lot of sulfur. As it's being digested, the sulfur turns into stinky hydrogen sulfide.

Other Snaky Stinkers

Pythons are not the only snaky stinkers ...

The copperhead pit viper eats mostly mice, voles, and sometimes frogs: no wonder its farts are dreadful. Reports say that when copperheads fart, they let out "a squeak ... so small that you think you may be mistaken ... until it hits you."

COPPERHEAD

Another snake it's best to avoid getting close to is the western hooknose. When surprised or scared, it starts thrashing around while at the same time pooping and farting. If you don't want to be splattered with snake poop, it's best to step away.

Do you speak Fart?

Humans don't communicate using farts. In the animal world, though, a fart can be worth a thousand words.

Time for some HISTORY ...

The Herring Fart (nearly) war

In the 1980s and '90s, Sweden's defense forces used sonar detection to pick up mysterious ticking and clicking noises in the sea near Stockholm Harbor. They thought the noises were coming from hidden Russian submarines. The Swedish prime minister sent an angry letter to the Russian president ...

The Swedish Navy prepared for battle ...

The two countries moved closer and closer to war ...

Then the Swedes realized that the ticking and clicking was actually being made by farting herring.

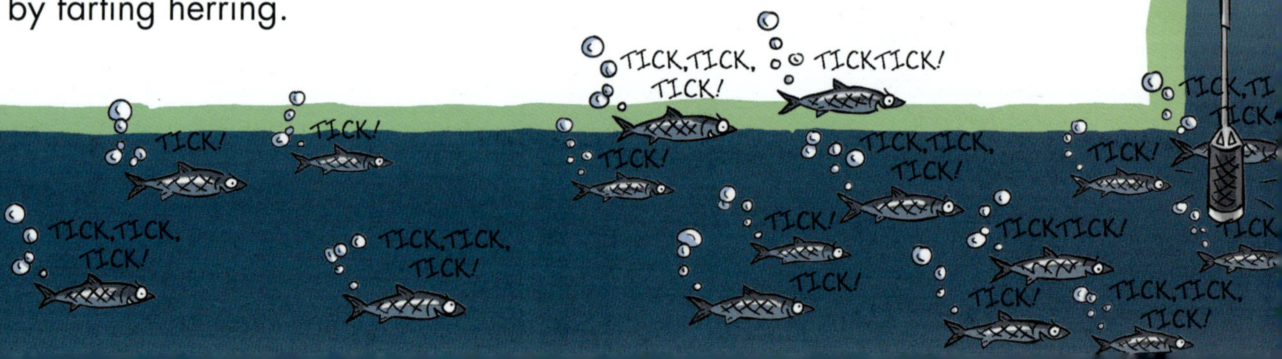

Herring farts

Experts think that herring use farts to help stay close together. They blow bubbles out of their bottoms, making a high-pitched ticking noise that only herring (and sonar operators) can hear. Scientists call this noise "Fast Repetitive Tick" … or FRT.

Herring use their FRTs as it gets dark, when they gather closer for defense. They also do more FRTs when they are moving: diving deep or rising to the surface. The herring seem to use the FRTs as a way of signaling that the school is on the move.

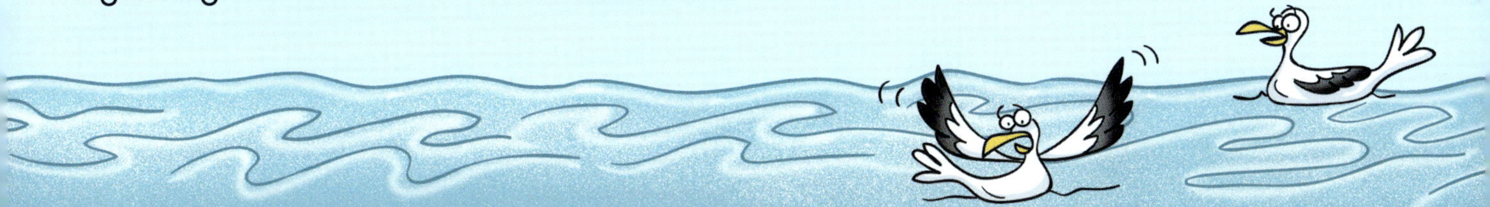

Time for some SCIENCE …

Gas and pressure

Gas is affected by a force called pressure. Pressure is linked to altitude.

High in the sky, pressure is low and gas expands to take up more space. (This is why people fart more on airplanes.) Deep under the sea, pressure is higher and gas is squeezed into a smaller volume.

In theory, a small herring fart released down in the depths would be MUCH bigger by the time it got to the surface (if it could make it all the way up).

watery FARTERS

Herring are not the only fish that fart. Our seas, lakes, and rivers contain lots of examples of watery farters.

The bolson ~~fart~~ *pup*fish

The Cuatro Ciénegas nature reserve in Mexico is home to animals that aren't found anywhere else on Earth. One of them is the bolson pupfish, which lives in shallow pools. The pupfish has a gassy problem:

1 Its favorite food is a kind of algae. In summer, the algae produce gas bubbles, which the pupfish swallows along with its dinner.

2 Gas builds up inside the pupfish. The little fish floats to the surface where hungry herons and other predators are waiting.

3 The only solution is ... FAAAAAART!

4 Once the fart has gone, the fish can swim down and bury itself in the mud, where it is safe.

Floaty farters

West Indian manatees are sometimes called sea cows. They spend a lot of time eating seagrass and plants from the seabed. Digesting the grass produces a LOT of gas, but the manatees have a use for it.

They can store the gas in pouches in their intestines, helping them float up when they need a breath. If they want to sink, they just let out a fart.

If a manatee can't fart like normal, it can cause problems.

The sand tiger shark is another floaty farter. Sharks normally sink to the bottom if they stop swimming, but sand tigers have been seen coming to the surface to swallow air. A sand tiger will then hold the air in its stomach, which allows it to hang in the water without sinking. Like manatees, when the shark wants to sink down, it just does a fart.

Deadly dog FARTS

Mr Pickles puts the "Poo!" in cockapoo.

Your family are sitting around the dinner table. Suddenly, someone sniffs and looks at the nearest person. "Was that YOU?" No – that's not human ... it was Mr. Pickles.

The biggest stinkers?

Anyone with a pet dog knows that they release some epic farts. As with humans, the smelliest dog farts are the ones with the most hydrogen sulfide gas.

Time for some SCIENCE ...

If there was ever a job that would make you NOT want to be a scientist, "dog-fart researcher" is it.

Nonetheless, some brave scientists have investigated what makes dog farts smelly:

1. Dogs wore a special suit, with a sulfur-gas detector located near the action zone.

2. An Odor Judge sniffed every fart (really) and gave it a score from 1–5:

1 = noise, no smell   5 = top-level smell factor

Wild stinkers

It's not just pet dogs that produce pungent pongs. If you value your nostrils, it's not a great idea to get close to African wild dogs or wolves.

African wild dogs live in packs and are very sociable. When members return from a hunt they all get highly excited, and start pooping and farting.

Wolves were the ancestors of all pet dogs (even teacup chihuahuas), so it's no surprise that wolf farts are pungent, especially given their meaty diets.

HOT AIR, OR NOT?

- There's a kind of puffball mushroom called a wolf fart.

NOT HOT AIR: This mushroom really does exist. It has a little hole in the top: when you squeeze the mushroom, it "farts" out spores.

- Hyenas are just giant, stinky dogs.

HOT AIR: Hyenas are not related to dogs at all! They are, however, very stinky. They eat only meat* and release nasty wind at the other end. The worst hyena farts are said to appear after camel intestines have been on the menu.

*Which gets caught in their teeth and rots, so they have bad breath too (not your biggest problem if a hyena's breathing on you ...).

FARTS and the END OF THE WORLD

The world's animals produce a LOT of gas. This stinky stream of gag-inducing gases is one of the causes of the climate crisis.

Cow farts: clobbering the climate

Cow farts (and burps) contain a greenhouse gas called methane. Some scientists think cows produce one-third of all the greenhouse gases that come from farming. Cow gases are adding to climate change at an alarming rate.

Time for some SCIENCE ...

Greenhouse gases and climate change

The farts animals produce contain a mix of gases. Some are greenhouse gases. They rise up into Earth's atmosphere and trap heat – like in a greenhouse.

The increase in greenhouse gases is one reason that global temperatures are rising. Animal farts are not the biggest source of greenhouse gases, but they are a significant one.

What can you do?

Many cows that are farmed for meat and milk would release *less* gas living in different conditions. How much gas they release depends on lots of things, including where they graze grass and whether they are fed a healthy diet.

You can help by eating less beef, but if you want to keep drinking milk, buy it from farmers who keep free-range cows or use organic farming methods.

Fighting the cow-gas menace

In 2016, the state of California decided to fight the cow-gas menace. It passed laws to limit the greenhouse gases escaping into the atmosphere from cow farts, burps, and poop.

Argentine researchers have collected farts in special "cow-fart backpacks," to measure how much methane a cow produces. The aim is to develop a new, less-farty diet for cows.

Some people have suggested using cow-fart backpacks to collect methane, then refining the gas to be used as clean fuel for things such as rockets or even to heat your house.

Weaponized FARTING

We know that elephants sometimes deliberately fart in each other's faces as a way of showing disapproval. And elephants are not the only animals to fight using fart power.

Fart facials 1

Elephants are big, which means they have big digestive systems and produce big farts. Elephants sometimes use these farts to show annoyance. If another elephant is really getting on their nerves, they turn around and give it a blast right in the face.

Fart facials 2

Sea lilies have no choice but to fart in their own faces. Their digestive system is U-shaped, and their anuses are right next to their mouths.

Moral: never sniff a sea lily.

Time for some SCIENCE ...

Farts that might fight infection

Farts don't have to be a weapon – they can be a good thing! In Singapore, researchers have discovered that chemicals in maggot farts have a special property. They kill bacteria that cause wounds to become infected.

YOU'RE WELCOME.

Polecat farters

Polecats and ferrets fart when they are scared. As well as farting, these creatures let out a high-pitched scream, puff up their fur and poop. All in all, it's best not to make a polecat or ferret nervous, especially as ferret farts are said to be very strong smelling.

Some people who own ferrets as pets even say that the animals surprise *themselves* with their farts: when the stink reaches their nostrils, the ferret gets a terrible shock and moves away.

FART LOVE

A human fart is enough to turn love into complete disgust – at least until the smell has gone away. Some other animals, though, find a fresh fart very appealing.

When a lady southern pine beetle wants company, she lets out a guff of gas. The fart contains a message:

The message is passed on using a chemical called a pheromone. It signals to nearby beetles that the female has found an excellent tree, and invites them to come and live there.

Time for some SCIENCE ...

Pheromones

Pheromones are chemicals produced by many animals. They are smelly messages understood by others from their species. Bees, for example, can smell-signal the need to defend the hive, tell female bees not to have young, or even tell a bee larva whether it should develop into a worker or a queen.

Baboons' bottoms

Insects such as beetles and bees aren't the only love-puffers. Female baboons operate in a slightly more visible way, though. When they are ready to mate, their hind quarters swell up. It's thought that the female's swollen bottom makes her farts louder and smellier. This is, believe it or not, very romantic and makes her extra-attractive to male baboons.

The female baboon with the biggest bottom is the most popular. Males sometimes fight over who gets to mate with her.

DO THEY or don't they?

The list of farting animals ranges from baboons to bobcats, tapirs to termites, and wombats to whales.
For some animals, though, the answer to, "Does it fart?" is ... we're not really sure.

Fartless Spiders?

Near the top of the list of maybe/maybe-not farters is the spider. This is because much of a spider's food digestion happens outside its body:

One thing is certain: if spiders DO fart, their farts must be tiny!

Blow-free bats?

Bats are mammals, a type of animal that also includes humans, elephants, dogs, seals, and other famous farters. You might think this means bats must fart too – but experts are not 100 percent sure. The reason is that bat digestion happens very quickly.

Bats need super-fast digestion because flying with a full, heavy stomach would be difficult. Just a few minutes after eating, the bat poops out what's left of its meal. Scientists are not sure how much digestive gas, if any, builds up in such a short time.

The woodlouse sort-of farts. Its digestive gas leaks out through gaps in its exoskeleton, rather than its bottom.

Fartless frogs?

Frogs MIGHT fart – some tadpoles are known to produce digestive gas, so frogs may too. They definitely don't make a farting noise, though. Frogs have very weak muscles around their bottoms. Any gas that did build up would just leak out, slowly and quietly.

FART-FREE animals

Imagine this: there are some animals that do not fart. These poor creatures will never know the pleasure of letting go of a stinker, then walking innocently away.

Shellfish without wind

One of the groups of fart-free animals is shellfish. Of course, they wouldn't be able to walk away even if they DID fart. The highest speed a young mussel or a clam can manage is less than an inch an hour.

Mussels anchor themselves packed close together on rocks, so it's probably a good thing they don't fart.

Oceanic non-farters

Because of underwater pressure, it would be a bad idea for some sea creatures to have lots of fart gas inside them. This may be why no one has ever seen an octopus fart, even though it has a slow digestive system.

No one has ever seen an octopus fart, but it's not because they are shy. Instead, experts think there are no fart-gas-creating bacteria in an octopus's digestive system.

Sloths: too lazy to fart?

Just about every mammal farts – except, scientists think, the sloth. Sloths have very, very slow digestion. It can take days for a meal to pass through their system. Instead of being farted out, scientists think the sloth's fart gas is absorbed into its bloodstream. It is passed to its lungs and breathed out.

Parrots: pretend farters

Lots of people claim that parrots fart. You might even have seen videos that seem to show parrots farting – except, they're not. We know this because, as far as scientists know, NO birds fart.

Time for some SCIENCE ...

Why don't birds fart?

There are two theories about why birds don't fart:

1. Like bats, birds need to be as light as possible to fly. Food passes through too quickly to produce large amounts of gas.
2. Birds do not have the kind of bacteria in their guts that release gas when digesting food.

Parrots are brilliant mimics. So when you hear a parrot "fart," it's making sounds it has heard regularly from its human companions ...

Did dinosaurs FART?

Birds are thought to have descended from a particular type of dinosaur, so this raises an important question: did dinosaurs fart if birds don't?

Dinosaur descendants

Most experts think that birds are descended from a group of dinosaurs called maniraptorans. Some of them even had feathers, including the famous *Velociraptor*.

Because maniraptoran dinosaurs were similar to birds, scientists think that they may not have farted. However, there were other dinosaurs that almost certainly DID pass wind ...

Stinker sauropods

The sauropods were large, plant-eating dinosaurs. Like modern herbivores they probably farted a LOT. And the sauropod *Argentinosaurus* was one of the biggest land animals ever to live – so you know what that means …

Time for some SCIENCE ...

Sauropod digestion

It's not possible to discover exactly what bacteria sauropods had in their intestines, because they died out nearly 70 million years ago. But experts think that the sauropods digested their food the same way cows do today – and cows definitely do fart.

Time for some more SCIENCE ...

Fart-powered climate change?

Experts have suggested that the methane farted out by large dinosaurs was similar to the amount we are adding to the atmosphere today. If this is correct, it could have caused rapid climate change.

Some people even suggest that climate change might have made dinosaurs extinct: the dinosaurs could not adapt to the new climate, or change their behavior to cool the climate, and so died out.

Animal fart EXTREMES

From the smelliest to the loudest, the longest to the smallest, here are some more of the animal world's extreme farts:

The Smelliest

No one yet has taken on the official role of "Animal Fart-Smell Judge." But there are a few animals whose farts are regularly said to be some of the worst things you can get up your nose, including rhinos and sea lions.

Time for some SCIENCE ...

Hind-gut digestion

Animals that eat a lot of grassy food often digest it near the end of their digestive system, called their "hind gut."

Because hind-gut digestion happens very close to the animal's bottom, gas builds up and escapes easily. Some of the world's stinkiest farters are hind-gut digesters, including horses, rhinos, and (experts think) sauropod dinosaurs.

Rhinos are contenders in three extreme-farter categories: 1. Everyone who has smelled a rhino fart agrees that they are terrible. They are also 2. really long and 3. very loud.

Sea lion colonies smell terrible – partly because of their dreadful fishy farts. Fish, shellfish and mollusks are just about all sea lions eat, so it's no wonder their gas smells so bad.

The loudest

The plains of Africa must be loud with the sound of farting! We know rhinos and hippos have tremendously loud, long farts, but possibly the most startling fart of all comes from the zebra. Its bottom belches can apparently be heard miles away.

Zebras fart loudly if they are nervous or when they start running. If a herd starts running because it is nervous, the farting must be truly impressive.

The longest

The record for the longest fart is almost certainly held by a human. Bernard Clemmens of London, England, is claimed to have done a fart lasting 2 minutes 42 seconds. Clemmens apparently needed treatment in a special air chamber afterwards because of all the gases he had built up in his blood.

Fast FART facts

- The Sonoran coral snake uses fart sounds to scare off predators. It sucks air into its cloaca, then fires it out with a pop-pop-popping sound.
- In 2015, smoke alarms on a flight from Australia to Malaysia caused an emergency landing. Investigators discovered that the alarms had been triggered by the farts of 2,000 sheep being transported on the plane.
- Every 24 hours, humans fart out nearly enough fart gas to fill a 1-liter bottle. Most people fart 5–15 times a day.
- Kangaroos don't fart that much – even when hopping. The bacteria in their guts produce less gas than other animals.
- Farts contain flammable gases. Normally, these just drift away into the air – but this does not happen in space. Instead, fans and filters have to be used to remove the harmful gases farted out by astronauts.

FURTHER FART INFORMATION

Bolte, Mari. Slimy and Smelly Animal Weapons and Defenses. North Mankato, MN: Capstone Press, 2025.

Chavez, Katie. Gross Animal Habits. Minneapolis, MN: Jump!, Inc., 2025.

Stiefel, Chana. How Rude!: Animals That Burp, Toot, Spit, and Screech to Survive. New York, NY: Union Square Kids, 2026.

Glossary

adapt change, to become suitable for a new purpose or situation

bacteria tiny living things made of only a single cell. Bacteria are present in soil, water, air, animals, and plants

climate change change in Earth's average temperatures to warmer conditions

climate crisis effects of climate change, which are leading to higher sea levels, melting polar regions, and changes in the weather

cloaca area at the end of the digestive tract

colony a group of animals or plants of one kind living close together

diet type of food someone eats. For example, the food typically eaten in the Mediterranean regions is often called a "Mediterranean diet."

digestion process of getting what the body needs from the food it eats

digestive tract part of the body where digestion happens

exoskeleton a hard covering on the body of some animals

extinct no longer alive

facial beauty treatment for the face

fart release or pushing out of digestive gases from the end of the digestive tract

flammable able to be set alight

greenhouse gas a gas, such as carbon dioxide or methane, that collects in the atmosphere and holds in heat

herbivore animal that eats only plants

intestine part of the digestive tract where most of the digestive process happens, also known as the gut

liquefied turned into liquid

methane colorless gas that does not smell

pressure force that pushes against an object

school group of fish

sonar method of detecting objects by sending out sounds and measuring their return

species group of living creatures that are similar to each other and are able to have young together

Sumerian from an ancient civilization that existed in the region of Mesopotamia, now southern Iraq, until about 2,000 years ago

volume amount of space an object takes up

Index

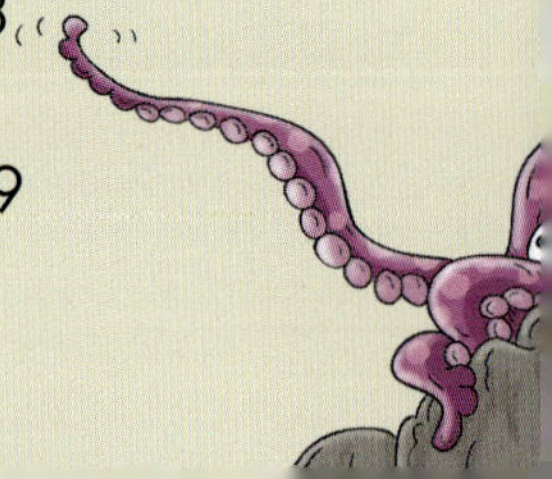